DROPSHIPPING

HOW TO LAUNCH A SHOPIFY STORE IN 1 HOUR AND MAKE $1000+ EACH MONTH WITHOUT INVENTORY

NOAH J. WALKER

TABLE OF CONTENTS

INTRODUCTION

Congratulations on downloading this book and thank you for doing so.

The following chapters will discuss how to start your own Shopify store, how to add products, and how to attract customers, so they buy your products. If you want to start your own online store with limited resources and no stock or inventory, then Shopify is the platform you need to get on.

You will learn how to market your Shopify store, how to receive payments and how to vet your suppliers. By reading this book and implementing the steps provided, you will be able to start earning profits within a matter of weeks.

There are plenty of books on this subject on the market so thanks again for choosing this one! Every effort was made to ensure it is full of as much useful information as possible. Please enjoy!

THE BASICS
OF DROPSHIPPING

What is Dropshipping?

D ropshipping is the process of selling products to customers through an online retail store but without investing in inventory. As a dropship entrepreneur, you first sign up with our preferred partner, AliExpress, and find a good supplier. Your AliExpress dropshipping partner will process orders from your customers and then ship products directly to your customers.

The ordinary retail trader spends a lot of resources buying products for their store. Stocking a store with inventory items is very expensive. A lack of money makes retail a tough business model for a lot of traders, especially those with limited resources. Fortunately, the dropshipping model enables such traders to start their own online retail businesses. Other terms that refer to dropshipping include:

DROPSHIPPING

- Drop ship
- Direct fulfillment
- Pack and ship

Why You Will Love Dropshipping

The business model that suits you perfectly is the dropshipping model because it gives you a chance to start your own business with very little upfront money. By adapting this model, you will be able to trade and make profits without buying stock for their stores.

Dropshipping provides you with one of the easiest models of starting a profitable online business. With no upfront investment required and with determination, you can easily start your own business, sell amazing products to customers and earn an attractive income even without handling any inventory. Processing orders and shipping are functions left to your dropshipping partners. Now all you have to focus on is carrying out the most important function which is marketing your business and finding new customers.

How Does Dropshipping Actually Work?

The dropshipping principle is really very simple. You first open an online store, find customers, and then start selling to your customers. Once a customer pays for a product at the store, the dropshipper proceeds to buy the product from a supplier who then processes the order and ships directly to the customer.

Here is a brief summary of the process.

1. First display your products professionally at your store

2. Customers will visit your store, view the products, place their orders and then pay for their purchases

3. Once you receive the money, you will use it to buy the products from your AliExpress supplier

4. The supplier then sends the product to your customer once they receive payment

Why the Dropshipping Model Is So Successful

- This model is successful because it puts you in control of your own profit margins on all products that you sell. Your AliExpress supplier does not dictate retail prices. This is a function that is left solely to your discretion.

- You do not need to be an established business to sell online. All you need to do is to setup your own Shopify store and start selling directly to customers. The process is so simple that you can literally get started right away.

- Once you set up your store, you get immediate access to millions of products from your suppliers. They do not have to process orders but leave all the processing and fulfillment to their partners.

The Buying and Selling Process Using Dropshipping Model

If you want to become a successful online entrepreneur, then you need to first set up your own Shopify store. The store should display your products beautifully and professionally. Make sure that you only display goods from your chosen suppliers. Your suppliers will provide you with display images and product information that you need.

When customers visit your store, they will view the products that you're selling then buy whatever they want and pay using the payment options provided. The money will then be instantly deposited into your account. Customers typically pay upfront for all the products they buy from you.

Once you receive the money into your account, you should immediately place an order for the products with your supplier. Orders are usually made online through the supplier's website or via an email. Your supplier will then charge you for the products, process the order, and finally ship them directly to your customers.

The package sent out to the customer will have your business address printed on it implying that it came directly from your store. This helps build customer loyalty which is important for your business. And that is it. Buying and selling products through the dropshipping model are very simple, clear, and straightforward.

Where to Find Dropshipping Suppliers

As a dropshipping entrepreneur, you should partner with a trusted supplier. While this sounds simple enough, it is not. There are plenty of untrustworthy individuals out there looking to scam entrepreneurs. It is important to find trusted companies and suppliers to work with.

The best approach to finding reliable suppliers is to use AliExpress verified suppliers. AliExpress is an established and trustworthy platform that provides convenience. Simply search for suppliers who meet the criteria set below.

We shall discuss more about AliExpress in Chapter 3.

Characteristics of an Ideal AliExpress Supplier

- The supplier has been on the market for at least 3 years

- Has made over 2000 sales

- Communicates very fast

- Speaks English reasonably well

- Has very positive reviews for the last couple of months

- Has very clear images of products

- Should have ePacket available for your product

Apart from looking out for trustworthy AliExpress suppliers, you also need to check prices so that your profit margins are assured. You should identify suppliers who price their products appropriately and allow you the chance to earn a decent profit. There are credible places and sites where you can find carefully selected and vetted suppliers.

You need to alert your supplier never to include any invoice showing product prices and not to include any advertisement in the package. I like to launch my online stores selling only to Canada, Australia, UK and USA using ePacket service. This helps avoid unnecessary shipping delays when goods are shipped from AliExpress. You should partner with suppliers who are 100%

reliable and will quickly fulfill and process all the orders they receive from you.

Getting Started with a New AliExpress Supplier

Once you identify a reliable supplier on AliExpress, you will have to contact them and sign an agreement that will define your relationship. This agreement is known as a reseller agreement. You can find it on your supplier's website. It will define a lot of important details such as how payments are processed, modes of communication, and so on.

You also need a tax number as a reseller and possibly a business bank account. These are easy to obtain and are often the first step of starting any business. Most legitimate dropship suppliers prefer to work only with entrepreneurs who are properly registered. Therefore, ensure that you complete this step before contacting suppliers. Once you sign the agreement, you can expect to be approved with a couple of days though it may sometimes take weeks.

Next Step after Signing up with Suppliers

Once you have your suppliers ready, you will need to import products into your website. By now, you should have a general idea of who your target market is and where to sell your products. Shopify is our ideal choice for this venture. We will use the app Oberlo to import products into your store.

It is imperative that you acquire all the relevant product images complete with description and other essential details such as price and so on. This information should then be organized efficiently so that customers can view products and related information with ease. This process is made very simple when you use Shopify together with the Oberlo app.

Important Things to Keep in Mind

- You must remember to do your marketing right. The only way to attract customers to your store is to market aggressively and advertise on different platforms. You should not just sit back and hope that the money will start rolling in. There are plenty of other entrepreneurs who are after the same customers so hard work,

and good customer service skills will get
you ahead.

- Another thing you need to keep in mind is
the pricing. Since dropshipping is a
competitive field, there are lots of other
entrepreneurs out there doing similar
business. If your prices are too low, then
you will not make enough profit, but if the
prices are too costly, then customers may
shun your store.

- Like most other businesses, profitability
and success largely rely on a number of
factors. If you manage your business
diligently, then success will come your
way. You can even be profitable from the
first month. Dropshipping is a great
business model with low risk and
excellent chances for great returns.
Remember that you have to dedicate time
and work hard at it. You will need to
market your business, add new products,
do your market research, engage with
suppliers, and all other essential
functions.

- If you have a long-term focus, have the
right business approach, and provide

excellent customer service, then you should not be surprised to start earning a six-figure income very soon. Getting to such levels might take some time, but it is very possible.

The Proper Mindset of a Successful Entrepreneur

- Sometimes things could go wrong. It is possible to make a mistake, and one of your choices could be wrong. At such moments, you may feel dejected, broken, hurt, and full of despair. However, you should NOT give up. Instead, examine your mistake. Try and find out what went wrong and what you could have done better. Then try again.

- If things appear not to be working out, simply check and confirm any information that does not add up. Alternatively, you can go to your favorite social media group and ask questions. There are plenty of useful Shopify tutorial videos on YouTube. You will definitely be able to find all the help that you need.

- Wherever possible, work with a dropshipping lifestyle coach. This is one of the best ways of ensuring that you are not alone in this journey. The coach will also help you avoid some of the pitfalls that most beginners encounter.

- Just remember that you will need to put in the hard work initially until your store gets known and you gain a number of loyal customers. You should never give up but instead remain focused and consult someone whenever you feel like giving up.

- Even as a beginner, you can still list your business on marketplaces and sell from multiple locations and in the process, earn thousands of dollars in sales per month. However, if you just sit back waiting for customers to visit your site, then you might have to wait for a long time. While regular retailers may seem more successful, their costs and overheads are much higher, so you are much better off as a dropshipper.

Common Dropshipping Mistakes

1. Too much worry about shipping costs

Shipping prices can be a cause for concern because they vary greatly from one region to another. However, you should not stress too much about this. Simply determine where your priorities are in this regard and then make a determination. It is easier to set a flat shipping cost so as to eliminate this stress.

2. Not providing easy access to order information

The information on your website will tell customers that the order process is simple, stress-free and orders are shipped out fast. Customers often want to see evidence. You should ensure that suppliers update you on order status and also provide estimates of shipping dates, so customers are informed.

3. Insufficient brand exposure

A lot of the time, you will forget to expose your brand so that customers keep seeing it consistently as they shop. Customers need to be reminded regularly and constantly about your brand so include your brand name and logo on as many pages as possible.

4. Messing up customer orders

This is another common occurrence. Customers often buy the wrong products or click on an item by mistake. Sometimes they place a legitimate order but later change their minds. If an order gets canceled, please inform your dropshipping supplier so they cancel otherwise you could end up with a bad rating.

5. Return complications

A lot of the time returns will occur, and most of the time they will be messy if not properly managed. You should put in place an elaborate system to handle returns. This way, you will avoid the stress associated with returns.

HOW TO PERFORM A PRODUCT & NICHE RESEARCH

It is said that the most successful dropshippers are the ones who perform a thorough niche and product research. There is no getting around this, and you just have to take time to research and identify the most profitable niches in the market. You can choose to sell your products to a niche market or to the general population

Dropshipping is a serious business which requires a trader who really knows what he or she is doing. One of the biggest challenges you can expect will be your choice of products to sell. If you get this right, then you will well be on your way to success.

Finding a Profitable Niche: Where to Start

A lot of traders recommend finding a niche that matches your interests and personal taste. While this sounds like a reasonable approach, it may not necessarily be the best. Do not rush the niche selection process. A lot of potential online traders often get it wrong at this stage and most never recover.

First of all, you need to know that you cannot start on a blank page. As it is, you already have your own thoughts about great dropshipping ideas. Think about products on Google Trends and look at the ones that inspire you or you are familiar with. Your mind is already full of excellent ideas so explore these within the context of dropshipping. Brainstorming is an excellent first step to make when identifying a profitable niche or product.

Google Trends is an excellent tool that can help you identify the best niche. It gives you invaluable insights into customers' interest in certain services or products. Google Trends is designed to help you analyze search trends, making it a useful service for your business. As a dropshipping entrepreneur, this tool will help you determine the following:

- The most popular search items on Google

- Changes of search volume over time

- Regions where the customers doing the search live

- Whether the interest in the search item seasonal or year round

You can also use Google Keyword Planner which is a popular tool for niche market analysis. When using this tool, ensure that you have as many keyword modifiers as possible, even when finding suppliers. Some of the keywords you can use include warehouse, supplier, reseller, wholesaler, distributor, and so on. Google Keyword Planner helps marketers and traders determine which searches can lead to your preferred niche market.

Experienced entrepreneurs will tell you that there are only two different kinds of niches. These are the good niche and the bad niche. The good niches are very profitable while the bad ones have very low margins. There are several ways of determining whether a niche is profitable or not.

Tools you can Use to find Trendy Products:

- https://thieve.co

- https://pexda.com

Good niches have the following characteristics:

- Plenty of sales

- Very little customer service required

- High-profit margins

On the other hand, bad niches have the following features:

- Very few sales

- Problematic sales

- Need plenty of customer service

- Low-profit margins

To be successful in identifying profitable niches, you need to allocate adequate time for your brainstorming sessions. Simply put everything else aside and concentrate on brainstorming.

First, prepare a list of about 50 excellent niches that have the characteristics listed above. Now examine this list using these criteria:

- *Loyalty*: Avoid products that are completely dominated by major brands

- *Weight:* Find products with low shipping weight (2kgs or less) because shipping is costly

- *Competition:* See what the competition is selling and avoid saturated products

Find products that are relatively costly because, the higher the price, the better the profit margin

- *Returns:* You should avoid products that offer size and style preference as customers are likely to return these at an alarming rate

Closely Examine Current Dropshipping Trends

Use eBay for your Research

You need to take a closer look at current trends in the dropshipping sector. One great way of doing this is to look at the trends in popular online marketplaces such as eBay. eBay is a great platform to check for products that sell well online. However, their prices are quite low so don't fix your prices based on eBay's pricing.

While on eBay, brainstorm with a focus on products that cost $500 or more. Expensive niches are preferable because you stand to make bigger profits compared with the less expensive ones. Browse through the different categories on eBay. Go and search through different categories then take a look at the results and thereafter alter the results to only indicate completed listings. The ones that are in red are the ones that did not sell while the ones in green sold well.

Use Amazon to Identify Specific Niches

Amazon sells pretty much every product in all niches. It is the world's largest retail outlet and can help you find profitable niches as well as products that sell really well. Here is the process of identifying profitable niches on Amazon.

1. Go to Amazon website and choose the "All" tab on the left side of the search bar. The tab will indicate an entire list of niches or categories

2. Now select a particular niche that you like, leave the search box empty and conduct an empty search

3. A new page will appear and, on the left, will be an entire list of sub-niches

4. Choose a particular sub-category that you like, and you will see additional sub-niches which are very specific

5. You can now examine these specific sub-niches and even go further if you like

Amazon is a great site to search for specific sub-niches and sub-categories. It allows you to find very specific niche areas that are lucrative and not overcrowded. You can also identify products in these sub-niches that sell extremely well. What's more, you can even use the navigation bar at the top of the page to find "Best Sellers" in various niches and categories.

At Amazon, you will always find a profitable niche and opportunities for great brainstorming sessions. The "Best Sellers" page is updated on an hourly basis and is, therefore, a completely reliable resource that you can use to find your preferred niche.

DROPSHIPPING

Take a Marketer's Approach

You should try to focus on selling products priced less than $4 but with a high perceived value. The reason is that it is much better to sell a low-priced item and sell hundreds of units to happy customers than deal with a high-value product and sell only 3 units a week. After all $3 * 200 = $600 is better than $30 * 3 = 90.

Also, it is much easier to convince customers to buy a low-price product than a costly one. Customers will be compelled to buy a useful product at $5 or less than $200 and above. You will find it easier to refund $5 to a disgruntled customer than $200. Therefore, start with low-cost products and focus on selling large volumes.

Competitors

Keep in mind that there are competitors within your niche. You need to check out their websites or online stores and find out how they price their goods. You will still probably not be able to know how much profit they are making. You can also use MAP to find out if a product is profitable. All you need to do is observe if a supplier enforces MAP policies.

Think "Barely" Out of the Box

When choosing a niche, most entrepreneurs fall into two main categories. There are those who choose very common niche ideas. Others choose very rare niches. The problem with popular niches is that they are often saturated. This leaves you in a highly competitive niche where selling is very difficult, and profit margins are limited. The very rare niches are outlandish and specialized. It is very difficult to make consistent sales in highly specialized niches. Avoid being either of these two entrepreneurs. Instead, opt for niches that are just outside the box.

A good example of this is a product like a portable ice maker. This item is not as common or popular as refrigerators yet not as rare and uncommon as a walk-in freezer. With this kind of reasoning and finding such sub-niches, you are likely to be very successful.

Watch Out for the Following Pitfalls

- Be careful about promoting common items that are regularly inspected and examined by customers. For instance, household electronics, technology, fancy clothing, and footwear are often inspected by customers before buying.

- Customers often try these items at the store before buying. Be careful about dealing in such products because you can expect tons of returns and even refunds. Your customers are also likely to experience challenges when choosing a product that they want. These are the kinds of challenges you want to avoid.

- Large, heavy, and bulky items pose shipping and handling challenges. At the very minimum, you are likely to experience a high cost of shipping such items. Your customers might even prefer buying such a product at the local, brick-and-mortar establishment. Try and avoid such bulky and heavy products.

- Also, be careful not to deal with fragile items that are likely to get damaged during shipping. Perishable or fragile goods such as ceramics, glass, and fresh produce are ideal candidates. You should avoid dealing with such products as well.

- There are products that can cause issues or problems in transit due to legal concerns. For instance, hunting knives, bows and arrows, swords, etc., are all considered dangerous or controlled. They require special licenses, and some transport and shipping companies avoid handling such goods. Stay away from such products if you can.

Here are some Benefits of Selling Niche Products

- Increased profits

  If you choose a well-defined niche, you will be able to focus on selling to profitable customers who promote your business. You can avoid customers that take up your money and time.

- Reduced marketing costs

  Niche products cater to very specific audiences. You really do not have to appeal to the mass market. This way, you will be able to market to an informed and passionate customer base that values the products and know what they want. This saves you a lot of costs as your marketing costs will be low.

- Less competition

  Basically, there are fewer businesses dealing in the niche area and niche products. Most deal in general products which they sell to the general public. Niche products allow you to gain market share and get a competitive advantage.

Niche Store versus General Store

Should you open a niche store or a general store? Niche stores have been aptly described above, and we have seen how much potential they have. A general store is a lot more like Walmart. Such stores tend to appeal to the general public and offer products for most customers within a particular genre such as fashion or kitchen appliances.

General stores tend to attract large numbers of visitors per day. Let's assume about 300 customers visit a general store with each customer spending an average of $2, then the store will generate revenues of about $600 in that particular day.

General stores tend to have a large variety of products to choose from. They contain lots of niches so customers can browse through a wide variety of products in different niches. It is generally easier to attract visitors to a general store than a niche store. General stores are useful in helping to determine successful niches. It will be up to you to decide which is better between a general store or a niche store.

Free Plus Shipping Model vs. Retail Price with Free Shipping Model

There are two successful pricing approaches that you can choose for your dropshipping store. You can either opt for Free Plus Shipping or Retail Price with Free Shipping. These are excellent strategies that will attract customers to your store and give you an edge over many other stores.

Free plus Shipping Model

The Free plus Shipping approach simply means you sell products at $0.00 but charge customers the shipping cost only. You may wonder how such a model will earn you a profit, but it actually works. All you need to do is adopt the approach of other dropshipping traders using this model. Just inflate your shipping costs little. This way, you will easily be able to cover the cost of the product and include your profit margins in there as well.

Let's take an example. A regular retail store may sell an item for $6 and then charge $2 for shipping for a total of $8. You can sell the same product at your store for $0, charge an $8 shipping cost and generate just as much revenue as the store. However, you are bound to attract more customers to your store than the average online store.

Benefits of the Free plus Shipping Model

- This model is very easy to start. It doesn't matter whether you are a seasoned trader or a beginner

- It is relatively simple to set up

- You can select from a wide variety of products

- Customers will love your store and will buy your products

- The shipping fees will seem like an attractive bargain

Be cautious, however, not to sell very cheap products and pay much higher shipping fees. For instance, if you sell a product worth $2 and charge $8 shipping fee, you might get into trouble if customers return the product. Also, be careful not to sell high-end products for a fee then charge high shipping fees. For instance, a free digital camera with a $50 shipping fee is bound to raise eyebrows.

Retail Price with Free Shipping Model

Another great dropshipping model approach is to offer free shipping to your customers. Customers love it when they do not have to pay any shipping costs.

However, as an entrepreneur, you can decide to factor in the cost of shipping into the product price, or you may be selling large enough volumes so that you can afford to pay the shipping costs.

Standard free shipping should not be an idea to consider because it takes a long time for goods to get to a customer. A better prospect is what is known as ePacket. While it is not free, it is a low-cost shipping option that you can successfully adapt if you use this dropshipping model.

For instance, an item costs 2.50 and shipping with ePacket is $2.00. You can sell this item at $24.99, charge zero shipping costs and still make sufficient profit for yourself and have plenty more left for marketing purposes. This is a great approach to free shipping model. It is considered unethical to charge shipping costs if your supplier offers free shipping with ePacket.

What is ePacket Delivery?

ePacket Delivery is a package delivery service through an agreement between Hong Kong Post and the United States Postal Service or USPS. The service allows for faster delivery of small packages weighing up to 2kg from Hong Kong and China to be shipped to the US and other countries.

Plenty of suppliers on Oberlo offer free shipping with ePacket delivery. Free ePacket is only available for the United States but with low-cost shipping charges to Australia, New Zealand, Canada, and the UK. You will have an advantage over other entrepreneurs if you offer free shipping service. Also, customers will be willing to pay a little more if you offer free shipping.

HOW TO SET UP
A SHOPIFY STORE

If you want to have your own presentable, unique, and high-quality e-commerce store with all essential features, then you need to set up a Shopify store. Without a doubt, Shopify is one the most popular online platforms that provide e-commerce solutions for entrepreneurs.

Shopify allows you, at minimal cost, to build a modern, functional, and professional-looking store all by yourself. The stores are very presentable and great quality. They are very similar to what any professional web designer would build.

What is Shopify?

Shopify is a premier e-commerce platform that allows entrepreneurs to create their own retail point-of-sale systems and online stores. It is a comprehensive, complete, all-in-one online trading solution. Shopify allows interested entrepreneurs to open an account and set themselves up. Once you open an account, you can do all the following:

- Design and create your online store by yourself

- Identify a variety of amazing designs to choose from

- Choose a catchy name and domain for your online store

- Add then display products complete with descriptions and prices

- Start receiving and processing orders from customers

- Begin handling payments through various payment solutions

- Decide if to run any promotions, give discounts, and sell products

In short, Shopify offers you a very cost-effective and affordable opportunity to create your own e-commerce business. The software on Shopify is constantly upgraded to make it more efficient and modern which makes it more reliable in the long term. As an account holder, you get to receive excellent customer support 24-hours a day, every single day.

Key Features of Shopify

Once you open a Shopify account, you will gain access to a wide variety of tools. These tools will enable you to set up and manage your business. There are different pricing plans offered by Shopify. Depending on the plan you choose, you will be able to access a variety of tools ranging from payments processors to themes and so much more. Here are some of these tools that you will gain access to:

- Paid and free apps from the Shopify app store

- Paid and free themes that you can access from the Shopify theme store to ensure your website is exceptional and outstanding

- Shopify's own payment processor to enable you to receive credit card payments

- Access to a blog that provides you with articles that guide you on how to successfully operate and manage your own business and connect you with customers

- Opportunities to grow and expand your business

- Enterprise plans for high volume entrepreneurs who prefer lower transaction fees

- Global experts who can advise and help design and market your online retail store

Open an Account with Shopify

The first step you need to do is open an account. Visit Shopify's website at www.shopify.com and find the Sign-up page. Open this page and follow the stipulated procedure to set up your account. There are a couple of details required and once provided, simply click on the link that says "**Create your Store Now**."

You need to come up with a unique name for your store. Shopify system checks all names you provide and only approves a unique store name. Other details that you will have to provide include your name, country of residence, address, and a contact number. Shopify also wants to know if you have products you wish to sell and, if so, which products these are. Once you provide all the necessary information needed for setting up your account, simply click on the tab "**I'm Done**."

If you are keen enough, you will notice that Shopify offers you a free 14-day trial once you open your account. This allows you to set up your store and test different things to see if and how they work without spending any money. At this stage, Shopify will require some details from you due to legal requirements. For instance, if you will be operating as a real store, then you will need to provide tax information and other relevant information.

Setting up your First Shopify Store

To set up your first store, you need to visit Shopify's homepage and look at the main dashboard. You will see plenty of buttons on the left-hand side. These include the following:

- Homepage button

- Orders

- Products

- Reports

- Discounts

One of the things that Shopify does is present you with an entire list of actions to take to fully set up, customize, and personalize your store before eventually launching it.

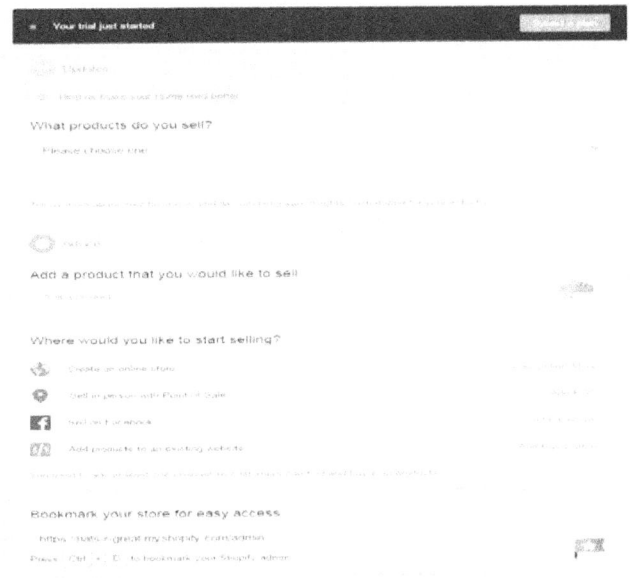

Shopify will then ask you what you want to sell. Simply choose one of the options available from the drop-down menu. These include electronics, computers, fashion, and apparel, and so on. Let us choose "Women's Accessories" like earrings, wristbands, and necklaces then proceed with this as our preferred niche.

At this point, you can start adding products to your store. The process is extremely simple. All you need to do is to click on an image then "drag and drop" it to the appropriate place on the dashboard. There is a button labeled "Add

Product" button that you click on to add products.

You should label your products in a manner that clients can identify with. This also makes things easier for you when uploading or referring to a particular product. However, many dropshipping entrepreneurs do not have their own products and rely on a dropshipping supplier. We will look at importing goods from suppliers later. However, if the product images are readily available, then you can upload using this simple method.

Once you are done, just click the "Save Product" button then go to the homepage to view the products. These products are now ready to be viewed and even purchased.

If you visit the dashboard of your homepage, you will be offered a couple of options. Shopify wants to know where you want to sell the products. You can choose to create an online store, sell on Facebook, sell in person with a Point of Sale system, or even add products to an existing website. From these options, we note that the most viable in our case is to create an online store.

Find a Suitable Layout or Theme for Your Store

One of the most important steps when setting up your store is choosing an appropriate theme. Shopify has its own themes, and you can browse through them and choose one. There are plenty of colorful, great-looking, and presentable free and premium themes that you can use.

Now, all the themes at Shopify come with a guarantee that they have full support from designers. This is reassuring for users, knowing they can fully trust the themes. All the themes have a comprehensive array of modifications that you can apply without the need to do any programming. Premium themes have more functionality, but you can still do a lot with the free ones.

If you choose a theme but wish to make substantial changes to it, then you need not worry if you cannot program. Apparently, Shopify has an excellent team of design experts from all over the world. These Shopify experts are available to members and can help you customize and make any necessary changes to your store. There are some pretty simple steps to follow if you are to find the best theme.

1. Browse the Shopify Theme Store

First, go to your homepage and then click on the "Themes" button. This button will take you to Shopify's theme store at www.themes.shopify.com. There are over 180 different themes to choose from. These include both free and premium themes. When browsing through the themes, you can choose to browse through the free or the paid themes.

You can also filter the themes by features and by industry. The themes can then be sorted by popularity, most recent, and price. Spend your time browsing through the themes until you find a couple that really impresses you. Do not rush this process because your interaction with your customers will depend on your store's outlook and presentation.

2. *Look at the reviews and functionality of themes*

Once you identify one or two themes, check out a sample image. When you do, you will also receive more information about the theme including its flexibility, adaptability, and responsiveness. Additional information lets you know whether the theme is mobile ready and how adaptable it is to modification. There are always reviews if you scroll down, so go and check out the reviews. These will let you know about the experience of other users and what their thoughts are on the particular theme.

Shopify has a cool feature that allows you to view any theme you choose in action. When you choose a theme, you will notice a "View Demo" button. Simply click on this button and preview the theme. This will give you a good feel of how your online store will look like. You can also view demos on the different styles if your chosen theme comes in a variety of styles.

3. Get your chosen theme

As soon as you decide which theme you like, you simply click on it to get it. You will notice a green button which you need to press. Shopify will want you to confirm that this particular theme is the one you really want. If you agree, then the theme will be installed. One advantage you have is that this theme does not have to be perfect. If you feel, later, that you do not like it, then you can always change it and choose another one. To install your chosen theme, simply click "Publish as My Store's Theme." Once it is published, Shopify will let you know and will offer you a chance to change it any time should you change your mind.

Top Free Shopify Theme

The theme that worked best for me is **Brooklyn**. It is among the most popular free Shopify themes available and comes in two different styles. These styles are Classic and Playful. The Playful style is more niche-oriented and features brilliant colors, making it suitable for kids' toy store, ladies fashion boutique, or even a chocolate store. The Classic theme is great for apparel stores and clothes retailers. It has excellent features, is user-friendly, and is very easy to use.

Brooklyn Shopify theme is well-suited for our modern apparel store. Some of its features include unique typography, product grid, homepage slideshow, and a mobile responsive design. It is not all themes that are designed to be viewed across platforms such as desktop PC, mobile, and tablet devices. You should not worry at all about products displayed on the theme as these are just for display purposes. You will get a chance to upload your own products at the appropriate time.

Edit Store Settings

You probably do not want your store looking like any other online store. This is why Shopify themes allow users to make simple yet effective changes that can completely alter your store's appearance. Consequently, you can rest assured that your store will be unique and stand out, depending on the settings that you choose.

First, visit your homepage and check out the admin screen. From here, click on "Themes" and you will see your live theme at the top. There are two dots next to the "Theme," both of which are settings that you can use. The first one allows you to create a duplicate of the current theme which is a great idea, so that is what we do. The other button is for customization. Use this button to customize the theme according to your preferences.

Simply click on the "Customize Theme" button, and you will be redirected to a page that allows you to manage all the basic functions of your Shopify store. These controls give you an amazing opportunity to adjust the settings and take a look at the features, enabling you to learn in greater detail what your store is capable of.

Customization allows you to change or do the following:

- Change font

- Determine the number of items to appear on each line on the collection page

- Upload logos to the store

- Determine your preferred color schemes

- Add slides to the homepage carousel

- Edit functionality on the product pages

With all these features and functions, you can easily make changes and adjustments to your store. This will make it unique, appealing and user-friendly.

Use Oberlo to Add Products to Your Shopify Store

Once you are done with the design and setup of your Shopify store, you now need to add products. For you to seamlessly import and add products, you will have to download Oberlo. It is the leading app used by e-commerce entrepreneurs who wish to import products to their stores. Shopify and Oberlo are seamlessly integrated, making it very easy to start importing and adding products to your store.

What is Oberlo?

Oberlo is a popular app from Shopify. It provides a useful service that enables you to import products from the popular Chinese store known as AliExpress. As a dropshipper, Oberlo is ideally one of the best applications available to you. Using Oberlo, you can easily and seamlessly import thousands of products from AliExpress warehouse and start selling to your customers.

The reason why Oberlo is crucial to Shopify dropshippers is that it saves them plenty of time and effort when adding products from AliExpress. Oberlo is currently being used in more than 6,500 Shopify stores and has more than 300 positive reviews. Oberlo works only with AliExpress and not any other wholesale stores or suppliers. There are some very good reasons for this so let us first teach you a little bit about AliExpress.

What is AliExpress?

AliExpress is a global wholesale, and retail online marketplace developed and overseen by Alibaba, the world's biggest online marketplace. Anyone can place an order for wholesale items on AliExpress. You can also purchase a single item and still be protected by AliExpress Buyer Protection.

Buyers on AliExpress can purchase products directly from manufacturers. This enables them to get lower prices as they cut out middlemen. Buying directly from manufacturers ensures that buyers and dropshippers are guaranteed the lowest prices in the market.

Most people describe AliExpress as the retail section of Alibaba which provides a useful service to millions of traders, retailers, and customers around the world. Alibaba on its own generates more sales than eBay and Amazon combined. The term express means that this service is designed for express, wholesale transactions.

The main target markets of AliExpress include small and medium-sized buyers and suppliers. This way, they are able to access high-quality products at very affordable prices. The minimum order accepted is a single item or product which is shipped via express delivery. Sometimes fast and free shipping is available to entrepreneurs.

Sign Up for Oberlo

There are two different ways you can use to sign up to Oberlo. The first is to visit the official Oberlo website at www.oberlo.com and sign up directly. The other option is to sign up through Shopify. The Shopify app marketplace listing makes it easy to sign up directly. The direct access is apps.shopify.com/ali.

In our case, we have already installed Shopify on our device so we will click on the installation link that is provided. This link is highlighted on the homepage and is easily noticeable. Simply click on it and register. Once the app is installed, it will appear on your homepage.

From here, you can begin adding products to your store. We will need to register a credit card on Oberlo to do a trial run. Please note that Oberlo is not free to use. You get a 30-day free trial on the premium plan before moving to the lowest plan which costs $4.90 per month. For the app to be activated, you will need to approve this charge.

Benefits of Using Oberlo

- The Oberlo dashboard is pretty easy to use. It also offers plenty of conveniences. You can access the Oberlo dashboard directly from the Shopify admin section. On the dashboard, there is a section labeled "Get Started" that helps you accomplish certain tasks. For instance, it helps you set up pricing rules so that you know how to price your products.

- Oberlo has plenty of simple video tutorials that help you understand how to set it up. For instance, you can watch tutorials that show you how to customize products, how to import them to your store, and even how to connect existing products. Always keep in mind that your products form the most important part of your Shopify store.

- Using Oberlo, you can search for products at AliExpress. There is a "Search Products" page where you enter different keywords to find the categories and actual products that you want. Oberlo also allows you to import products to your Shopify store using either the product ID or products URL.

- You can also use Oberlo's Chrome extension if you want to import products as you browse AliExpress. If you are lacking ideas, then you can access a featured products page to get ideas. Sometimes you have to search through numerous products to find the right one. Each product comes with important information such as product rating, price, sales figures, supplier information, and so much more.

- Now that you have uploaded all the products to your store, you are ready to begin selling. Making sales and generating revenue are really what your Shopify store is all about. However, you will still have a lot of work to do because by simply launching your store, you will not necessarily attract any significant traffic. Therefore, you will also need to engage in suitable marketing campaigns to bring in potential customers. Keep trying different marketing methods until you find the one that works for your business.

Other Must-Have Apps for Shopify

1. Free Shipping Bar by Hextom

Free Shipping Bar is an app that provides a fully customizable bar. It enables you to offer free shipping to your customers to increase your sales. This app is easy to set up. It is not branded making your site look organized professional. It is an app that you definitely need for your store.

2. SalesPop

SalesPop is a powerful tool that helps you boost your sales. It is estimated that over 85% of store visitors never buy anything. Reasons for this include store authenticity, trust issues, engagement and so on. SalesPop helps create an aura of a busy store which will entice customers to actually buy products at your store.

3. *MailChimp*

This is a useful marketing app with multiple applications. This app helps you capture emails from visitors and then create a marketing list. You can then use the list created to send marketing messages, newsletters, and so much more.

4. *Personalized Recommendations App*

This is an e-commerce app for Shopify that promotes sales at your store. It suggests the right products to customers based on purchase history and behavior. The app can tailor recommendations to every unique customer to your store.

5. *Countdown Cart*

This app helps create urgency in customers. A lot of customers tend to delay buying. However, Countdown Cart helps convince buyers to go ahead and purchase products at your store.

6. Trust Hero

This app boosts the level of trust that customers have in your store. When you have this app activated, it will display trust icons at your store and reduce incidences of cart abandonment. Customers will gain trust in your store and will be happy to buy your products.

There are websites like hotjar.com where you can create heatmaps and see how visitors are using your site. You can collect useful feedback which you can use to turn visitors into customers. It also enables you to know if your site has errors.

DROPSHIPPING PRODUCT PRICING STRATEGY

D ropshipping is a business model and e-commerce trend with high-profit potential and relatively low efforts. To be successful, you really should have a sound pricing policy. It is imperative that you determine your dropshipping pricing policy appropriately.

As a dropshipper, your only source of revenue is the difference between the prices offered by the suppliers and the prices that you set. This difference is crucial, so you need to make sure that it is well thought out. You also need to ensure that you price your products right to be successful.

Getting the Price Right

Every entrepreneur grapples with the challenge of pricing their products. A good pricing strategy enables you to understand the point at which you can maximize your profits based on the sale of your products. Ideally, when you consider all the essential factors, you should be able to easily make the correct decisions and price your products appropriately for maximum profits.

Of course, at this stage, you still have plenty of questions on your mind. For instance, you may wonder how to determine the fair price of a product and how to find out the real value of a product in your store. There are a number of important factors that you will need to consider. Such factors include your customer base, the competition, as well as your distribution costs.

Pricing Strategy for Your Shopify Store

What is a pricing strategy? This is a method that you use to price your products appropriately. The price strategy aims to enable you to maximize profitability while maintaining your customers. Pricing offers you the most efficient way of optimizing your store's potential. If you apply a good strategy, your store will remain profitable, efficient, and long-term sustainable.

On the contrary, if you do not use a proper strategy to determine your pricing, then you will get into trouble. You might price your products too high or too low. This will cost you because you may lose customers who will seek lower prices elsewhere or you may not make sufficient profits to remain in business. Your customers may even suspect your products to be of poor quality.

The reason pricing is so important is because it is one of the major decisions that customers have to consider when shopping online. It is believed by consumer research firm PWC that most customers visit online stores just to compare prices. Other reasons include participate in promotions or to find coupons. In general, customers are always searching for great prices and, when applicable, discounts, vouchers, and coupons.

Best Dropshipping Pricing Guidelines

1. *Find products that cost less than $4 if you can*

   It is much easier to convince customers to purchase a product that is worth $4 or less compared to a pricier one. For instance, it is easier to convince a customer to purchase beautiful earrings that look great on her, match different outfits and cost about $2.75 that sell her a designer bag worth $400.

2. *Give customers discounts, offers, coupons, and deals*

Everybody loves discounts, deals, and offers. The best approach is to keep your prices high at the beginning. Then, once you feel like you are no longer a new entrepreneur and are established, you can offer discounted product prices and coupons. These awesome deals can be offered to your customers. It will result in hordes of new customers visiting your online store regularly. Therefore, varying your prices a little can prove to be an excellent pricing technique for your online business.

3. *Aim for zero shipping costs*

As an online entrepreneur, you want to find products that have no shipping cost whatsoever. Ideally, you should mark products on your site as close to cost price as possible. Customers dislike shipping costs and will try to avoid these whenever possible. Find suppliers who provide free ePacket services. Many of them do so try to find one who is trustworthy within your niche.

4. *Flash the psychological card*

It is common practice by retailers to use odd numbers because customers prefer prices ending in odd numbers. Try to always mark your prices with odd numbers at the end such as $5.99. Your customers will round off this figure as $5 and not $6. While this may seem a bit strange, it is a strategy that works. You should implement it at your store and see how well it works.

5. *How to handle returns*

You will definitely love it anytime you sell and make a profit. However, returns will really bother you. Returns are always depressing for dropshippers. However, this disappointment can be a blessing in disguise. Always try to assist the customer where necessary. Focus on making the customer happy and avoid getting stressed. If your customers are happy, they will come back and will be happy to pay higher prices in future.

6. *Choose products with multiple variations*

It is important to identify a product that comes in different variations. This makes it easy for customers to choose as they love variety. It also works pretty well with the Free with Shipping cost model.

7. *Use Simple but Powerful Phrases*

It is important that when pricing your products, you make use of powerful phrases. Such phrases have a powerful impact on customers and will entice them to buy your products. For instance, use phrases like, "Get your adorable wristbands for FREE for a limited time only. Simply pay for Shipping!"

You should also let the customer know how long it will take before receiving their products. This revelation is essential for as a sales strategy. You can let them know that it will probably take 4 to 7 days for delivery. Customers love it when they have this information upfront.

BEST PROMOTION
STRATEGIES

Once you have created your store, identified your products, and priced them appropriately, you now have to drive traffic to your store and thereby get customers to buy your products. It is important to promote your products and the store on different platforms using a variety of methods. You need to do this regularly whether you are seeking your initial sale or have been in the business for a long time. It is always advisable to identify more ways of marketing your products.

There are many different and creative ways of promoting your products. We need to find the most suitable and effective marketing techniques and use them to attract customers to your store.

- Email marketing

- Print media ads

- Facebook shop section

- Reddit advertising

- Affiliate marketing

- Instagram

- Pinterest

- Facebook audiences

- Blogging

- YouTube

- Gift guides

- Pop-up shops

Open a Pinterest Account

Pinterest is one of the most effective marketing platforms for selling your products online. Many Pinterest users, up to 93% of them, claim that they would use the platform to find products to buy and services to use. This makes it an excellent platform to advertise your products. It is a free platform that is very popular with users, so it is imperative that you open an account there and reach out to the thousands of active users.

Use Social Media to Reach Out to New Customers

1. How to Work with Social Media Influencers

Sometimes, updating social media sites and writing blogs can feel pointless if you have a pretty small audience. One way of getting a pretty large following and numerous sales leads is to connect with influencers.

Basically, influencers are websites or individuals with numerous followers online. The following could be on social media or niche websites. Basically, one message, tweet, or post about your products will send a huge flood of potential customers to your store.

How to Identify Influencers

A lot of time, new entrepreneurs are unsure how to identify influencer to contact them. Influencer marketing is a form of marketing that places the focus or emphasis on specific individuals rather than the target market. It is advisable to search for micro-influencers with 1000 to 10,000 followers within a niche than celebrity influencers.

You can use apps such as BuzzSumo to identify influencers in your niche. BuzzSumo is a powerful app that searches for key influencers on Twitter in any topic area, niche, and location. Once it identifies the main influencers within a certain niche, it follows them and then adds them to your Twitter list. You can choose to follow probably three or four of the major influencers. You will then be able to see what kind of content they share, review the information they share, and even read their posts. If you are happy with the influencers you find, then you can proceed to contact them.

You can also use the app Pitchbox to instantly find influencers in a given niche. Our niche is women's accessories so we can use Pitchbox to find influencers who are popular in this niche. Using this app, you can identify important influencers without any manual input and then send them customized emails. Those who do not respond to your emails will be followed up.

How to Contact Influencers

1. Use video message to contact influencers

Getting noticed by influencers is rather challenging because they receive numerous messages, likes, and tweets from many of their followers and even entrepreneurs. You really need to think out of the box to catch their attention. For instance, you can create a superb video message and send it to an influencer as a direct tweet. Take the case of Aaron Orendorff, a respected social media influencer. He receives thousands of messages daily but a video tweet from an entrepreneur caught his eye, and they got talking.

2. Send influencers a personalized Boomerang message

Another great way of interacting with influencers is to send a personalized Boomerang message on Twitter. Boomerang is a free app from Instagram that allows you to send an animated GIF to anyone on Twitter. The app takes 4 of your photos and converts them to a 4-seconds looping GIF.

This is also bound to catch the eye of influencers.

3. *Share and then tag an influencer to his or her content*

You should find an influencer's content and then share it with your followers. Remember to tag the influencer to the shared content. This is such an effective way of catching their attention yet only very few people use it.

4. Follow and engage an influencer regularly

Twitter is a pretty noisy platform with lots of tweets, posts, and messages. It is difficult to regularly keep up with an influencer or engage them. Fortunately, you can catch their eye by engaging their content frequently. You should read and respond to their posts at least once a day. This can sometimes be tedious and time-consuming so you can use Twitter lists. A Twitter list is a great way to find Twitter users' content and engage with the influencers. You can easily create a list of influencers by going to their profiles and adding them to your list using the drop-down menu.

How Much are Influencers Paid?

Influencers are crucial in any serious marketing venture. They are used by large brands and small traders alike to attract customers to their products and online stores. About 85% of Americans somewhat or totally trust recommendations and endorsements from people they know. It is always a challenge to work out how much to pay influencers.

DROPSHIPPING

The first step is to define your store's objectives and goals in partnering with an influencer. Do you wish to rent an influencer's audience? Are you looking to form a long-term relationship that may include co-creating content? Does the influencer have a reasonable audience within your preferred niche?

All influencers are not the same and some command bigger followings than others. Those with more than 250,000 followers definitely command a higher fee than those below that. Micro-influencers may not have as many followers but definitely engage their followers a lot more and with more useful content. Here is a list of average earnings for influencers

- Micro-influencers with less than 1000 followers earn $85 per post

- Influencers on average earn $270 per post

- Those with over 100,000 followers earn $765 per post

However, these figures are not cast in stone, and you can always negotiate with any influencers you wish to work with. Negotiated agreements tend to have a greater impact on your niche market than the general agreements.

Instagram Influencers

- Instagram influencers are crucial to any business. Their marketing messages are subtle, so they don't feel like advertisements. Influencers are a great choice for your preferred business or niche because they post ads that don't seem like ads.

- Find influencers who are the right fit and resonates with your business. This way, their story will resonate with yours. Such an influencer should also have followers who are potential customers. Therefore, start by determining who your target audience is. Focus on location, gender, attitude, social standing, age and similar factors.

- Your preferred influencer should be interested in your product and should have the same interest as you do in your niche or area of specialization. Sharing interests with an influencer is extremely important for your business.

- You need to choose between a micro and macro influencer. Micro-influencers often focus on a small niche but have very loyal followers. Macro influencers have much larger followings. Think about your store and its products and you will know who your preferred influencer is.

- A crucial factor that you need to consider is the number of followers. A suitable influencer needs to have between 200K and 300K followers. Also, each of their posts should have high engagement with followers. When you identify such an influencer, see if they have ads on their page and how these ads are faring.

- Influencers charge for their services. However, you need to be savvy and bargain for a fair price. Basically, you should not pay more than $25 to $30 for a 24-hour post.

Now you are ready to contact the influencer. Simply send a message directly to the influencer and let him or her know about your marketing needs. Make sure that you agree on the price as well as the date. The best day to have your marketing message or post marked is Sunday. Once this is agreed, prepare the ad and then send it to the influencer. Provide a catchy description and also a direct link to your products.

2. Make Use of Facebook

There are two different ways to use Facebook as a marketing tool. You can opt for Facebook Custom Audiences or Facebook Shop Section. Facebook is accessed by hundreds of millions of users each and every day. The Custom Audiences offers an excellent way of marketing to a select audience. Your ads will be targeted to your website visitors and email subscribers. This method is very effective.

An alternative or additional tool that you can use is to open a Facebook Page and add a Shop Section to it. Using your Shopify store, you can use Facebook as a sales channel and create your own Shop Section. This will attract plenty of fans and friends who then buy directly from your Facebook page.

How to Set Up Facebook Pixel

Facebook Pixel is an app or tool from Facebook. You need to insert this app into your website so that it tracks the conversions originating from Facebook. It also helps you to optimize your ads based on the data collected. Facebook Pixel works by triggering cookies which it places on your visitors that track users who interact with your Facebook ads and your website.

How to Create your own Facebook Pixel

1. Go to your Facebook Ads manager and select "**Pixels**" from the drop-down menu.

2. Choose "**Create Pixels**" then go ahead and create the Pixel.

3. Give your Pixel a name, agree to the terms and conditions and proceed.

4. Now add the Pixel to your website so that it is activated. You will also need to add some code to your web pages. Simply copy paste the code or use the Tag Manager. All these are accessible from Facebook Ads Manager.

5. Now just confirm that your Facebook Pixel is working properly.

How to Set Up Google Analytics

Google Analytics provides a free and simple method of tracking and analyzing all visitors to your store. Google Analytics helps find out who these visitors are and what they are looking for. Here is how to use it to help improve your

1. First, sign in to Google Analytics using your ordinary Google account.

2. Find the Admin button on the sidebar then create an account.

3. Create a property using the drop-down menu.

4. Then choose a website and add your store's name and web address or URL.

5. Select your time zone and indicate your industry.

6. Get a tracking ID then install it on your website.

DROPSHIPPING

Once your account is set up, you will have access to various reports including organic search visitors, keywords used to find you, the source of your landing page, and even active users. You should read these and other reports that will be generated by your Google Analytics account.

FACEBOOK AND INSTAGRAM MARKETING

Facebook Advertising

You should open a Facebook Page for your store and advertise your products on your page. Facebook advertising is one of the most important and influential online advertising methods you can use. By using Facebook, you can target your advertisements based on gender, interest, and even age. For our Shopify store, such targeted ads are absolutely essential. Established advertising networks like Google Adwords and Yahoo are both not able to target customers using such demographics.

There are generally four different types of Facebook ads that you can use. These are:

- Marketplace ads
- Page Post ads
- Sponsored Stories

- Promoted Posts

Selling your products on Facebook gives you a high chance of selling incredibly well. One of the best approaches that you should use is direct sales. However, there is a process we need to follow to determine the best campaign.

1. We first determine our products. In this case, our products are the latest women's accessories

2. We then determine our demography which includes both male and female aged 18 – 49 years, small firms, and institutions

3. A suitable image needs to be identified

4. Then create a compelling advertisement

5. Now let this ad run for two weeks

Marketplace ads are common on Facebook and are preferred by small entrepreneurs including first-time Shopify entrepreneurs. These ads will drive customers to your store, and you will very possibly make great sales. However, if direct sales using Facebook marketplace ads do not quite work out for you, you may try out another one.

Setting up Facebook Ads

1. *Start by identifying a hot selling product for your Shopify store*

   This is an important starting point and the most crucial aspect of Facebook Ads. Bad products will result in no sales even with great ads. However, a great product with decent ads will generate sales. Ensure that your products are in high demand and people are buying these products.

2. *Targeting is the next most crucial step*

   When it comes to Facebook Ads, then targeting is the next most crucial step. It refers to the actual audience being shown your Facebook ads. So a great product targeted at the right audience is going to generate sales for your store.

   Insert Ad Manager on your Facebook Page

   This is the easiest way of finding the right product and getting a targeted audience.

Facebook will give you tons of options, and you will need to choose the most appropriate one for your store. Allow Facebook to give you options for your product. You must make sure that you select the right product.

3. *You will need to Conduct Split Testing*

Split testing is necessary if you are to find the right kind of audience. The first option for this testing is to use the 3 X 3 testing. Here you will have 3 different ads running at $5 a day for three days. These will target 3 different audiences for 3 days. This is the fastest way of identifying your audience.

If, for instance, you are marketing a flashlight, you would create one ad set that targets campers, another one that targets those who love the outdoors, and one targeting travelers. Note that the ads are all the same and the only difference is the target audience. You will notice in time that one ad is likely to outperform others. You can split the sets further into age sets. You may find that one age set is a lot more profitable than all the others.

Creating Facebook Ads

You need to take the product, create an ad then post the ad on Facebook. So first find the product and then copy a large image of the product and go to Canva. Canva use for Instagram is described below.

Go to Facebook Ads and insert the image then size it. Give the product a nice name and use a suitable color for the background. Doing all these on the Facebook Ads Page is easy.

Make use of powerful marketing strategies of creating either a scarcity or urgency. Scarcity approach may indicate that the product is only available at that price for the next 100 customers only.

You can also create urgency. For instance, you can let a customer how lucky they are because, just for that day, the product will be available at a given price. For instance, a beautiful bracelet will cost $3.50 just for today.

Remember to include product details so your targeted audience can view the ad and get all the information they need about it. A clear image and sufficient information will ensure customers know exactly what they are buying.

Depending on the selling model you use, such as Free + Shipping or Free shipping, use this to entice customers. For instance, you can say, "You can get our best selling bracelet for free, today only. Just cover the shipping." Do not ask customers to pay for shipping. Use the word cover. This is a powerful sales message that you can use.

Review your Facebook ad and if you are happy with it, just go ahead and post it. Then review its performance after three days. Remember to post the link to your product once you finish writing the marketing message.

Set Up Your Instagram Profile for Your Shopify Store

Instagram is one of the top social media sites and is very popular with users around the world. Users prefer Instagram because it is designed specifically for sharing photos and videos.

Instagram is also widely used to attract customers to businesses so if you want to succeed as an entrepreneur, then you should have an Instagram account. Opening an account is a pretty simple and straightforward process. Simply go to the website's homepage at www.instagram.com and then open an account. However, if you want a compelling Instagram business account for your e-commerce store, then use apps such as Canva, www.canva.com.

Canva allows you to create compelling and outstanding social media pages to set you apart from the rest. Canva has excellent tools that allow you to drag and drop images and photos to create an impressive page.

Create a Catchy Instagram Story to Impress Customers

You can use Canva and Instagram Stories to share videos and images that last an entire day. Instagram Stories provides an excellent platform for sharing images of special occasions, for daily updates of your store and products, and even for presenting special offers.

You are also allowed to post images from your phone's or computer's library. This simply means you are not just limited to posting images and videos from your camera. This allows you to be as creative as possible using all sorts of content. With the drag and drop tools offered by Canvas and their incredible media library, you will be able to easily create an eye-catching, unique, and impressive posts which you can share with your customers.

How to Open an Instagram Account

Opening an Instagram account and verifying it is a very simple process. You can sign up for a new account using your Shopify e-commerce store or simply log into Instagram using your Facebook account. Simply go to the Instagram homepage at www.instagram.com to start the process.

Once you sign up, you will be prompted to add a profile picture. If you are creating a Shopify page for Instagram, then the best choice will be your business logo. This will enable you to achieve a high level of branding. The more users see your logo, the more they learn to identify with it. This will enable customers to think about your store whenever they want to shop for women's fashion accessories. Remember that you only get 155 characters to describe your profile picture so use an image that is worth a thousand sales.

How to Use Canva to Create an Instagram Story

Start by opening a Canva account by visiting www.canva.com. The process is again very easy and straightforward and takes only a couple of minutes to complete. This is essentially the starting point of creating powerful and memorable Instagram Story posts.

Once your account is live, visit the library at Canva and select one of the many professionally created templates. As soon as you have chosen your preferred template, you can then upload your own photos or select your preferred one from over a million stock photos in the library.

Now, you are ready to prepare your Story so attach the images then add impressive filters and edit the text. Finally, save the Story and share it on Instagram. It is that simple. You will be able to present your viewers with stunning images and fantastic videos which are quite impressive and memorable.

Canva is a very easy to use program. It allows you to make changes to images, fonts, colors, and background very easily. The Canva platform offers you a great opportunity for promoting and advertising flash sales, short-term offers and even for telling your story. Canva is easy to use, fast, and very convenient. It gives you an edge, as a trader, over other entrepreneurs.

CONCLUSION

Thanks for making it through to the end of this book! Let's hope it was informative and able to provide you with all of the tools you need to achieve your goals whatever they may be.

The next step is to start implementing the various processes described in this book. You should be able to easily open a Shopify store and find products on AliExpress to sell to your customers. If you follow these steps precisely and accurately, then you should be able to start making money after only a few days.

Finally, if you found this book useful in any way, a review on Amazon is always appreciated!